MW00950357

Marco Polo

The Boy Who Explored China
Biography for Kids 9-12
Children's Historical Biographies

BABY PROFESSOR

EDUCATION KIDS

Speedy Publishing LLC
40 E. Main St. #1156
Newark, DE 19711
www.speedypublishing.com

Copyright 2017

All Rights reserved. No part of this book may be reproduced or used in any way or form or by any means whether electronic or mechanical, this means that you cannot record or photocopy any material ideas or tips that are provided in this book

In this book, we're going to tell you about the amazing life of the explorer and traveler Marco Polo. It's an exciting story, let's get right to it!

WHO WAS MARCO POLO?

Marco Polo was an explorer who traveled throughout China and the Far East. At that time, very few Europeans had been to China, so the stories Marco Polo wrote helped people in Europe to understand the Far East.

MARCO POLO

WHEN DID MARCO POLO FIRST TRAVEL?

Marco Polo was born in Italy in the town of Venice in 1254. At that time, Venice was a very wealthy city that specialized in trading. It was a hub for imports and exports.

At the age of 17, Marco traveled to China with his father and uncle. They had been there before and had been introduced to the famous Mongol Emperor Kublai Khan who was China's leader. They had promised Kublai Khan that they would return. When they left, Marco had not yet been born. When they finally got back to Venice, Marco was 15 years old so he only knew them for two years before they traveled together.

Marco Polo

Silk Road

WHAT WAS THE SILK ROAD?

During this time, silk was one of China's major exports. The Silk Road was the name for the routes that traveled from Eastern Europe to the northern region of China. Along the way, there were major city centers as well as trading posts.

Because it was a very far distance, not many merchants traveled the entire way. It took a long time before products were transported from one section of the route to another.

Marco's father Niccolo and uncle Maffeo had an innovative idea. They wanted to travel to China themselves and bring the products back to the city of Venice. They thought it would make them wealthy if they could cut out the middlemen along the way. They traded rare items, such as silk, spices, and gems. However, they didn't realize that this first trip would take them fifteen years from Venice to China and back. There were no trains or airplanes back then.

Ships used by the Polos

WHERE DID THE POLOS TRAVEL?

After traveling for about three years, Marco and the two elder Polos arrived in China. They visited great cities all along the way. They saw the sacred city of Jerusalem and the Hindu Kush mountains in Asia, as well as the country of Persia. They even traveled through the Gobi Desert. They were introduced to many different cultures and had exciting adventures.

LEARNING THE CHINESE LANGUAGE

Because Marco, his father, and his uncle lived in China for so many years, they eventually learned to speak the language. They were employed by the Great Khan as messengers, and Marco formed a strong friendship with Khan. Marco went on special missions as Khan's messenger, tax collector, and sometimes spy.

1254 MARCO POLO 1954
PAX TIBI MARCE
歐亞聯璧
POSTE
LIRE
60
REPUBBLICA ITALIANA
IST. POL. STATO OFFICINA CARTE VALORI ROMA

Having the emperor's trust and protection allowed all of them to move freely without fear within the borders of the Mongol Empire. Marco even traveled as far south as where the country of Vietnam is today. He was given a special golden tablet that gave him permission to use the emperor's horses and lodgings. All the Polos were considered to be the emperor's honored guests.

KUBLAI KHAN'S COURT

The immense wealth of the emperor's court fascinated Marco. He had never seen anything like it in Europe. The capital city of Kinsay was very large but it was also clean and orderly compared to other large cities he had seen. Huge construction projects such as the very wide roads and the Grand Canal were far beyond similar construction projects in Italy and the other countries he had traveled.

Creating Pasta

ADVANCED CHINESE TECHNOLOGIES

There's a common misconception that pasta didn't exist in Italy until Marco brought it back from China, but that's not true. Pasta had already been around for centuries. However, there were some inventions that Marco described in the book he wrote upon his return that hadn't yet been seen in Europe.

Paper money, coal, and possibly eyeglasses were some of the inventions that the Chinese had that Europeans did not. Marco also described in detail the vast number of checkpoints as well as couriers that the Great Khan used to communicate within his huge empire.

Coal

MYTHICAL CREATURES OR NOT?

After he came back from his travels to China and the Far East, Marco wrote about what he had seen, but sometimes his writing wasn't entirely accurate. He didn't really know how to describe monkeys, elephants, and crocodiles, for example. He described the crocodile as a huge, sharp-clawed snake that could swallow a man in one bite. He sometimes confused the animals he had seen with mythical beasts, such as when he described the rhinoceros as a one-horned unicorn!

DID MARCO MAKE IT BACK TO EUROPE?

The Polos made it back to Europe, but their trip was perilous. After years of traveling and coming close to death several times, when they were ready to go home, the emperor was old and didn't want them to leave.

MARCO POLO

Eventually, he let them leave in 1292 to escort a Mongol princess on a sea voyage. This was the most dangerous part of their travels. The princess survived the voyage and so did the Polos, but many others did not and hundreds died before they reached the port of Hormuz in Persia.

Once they were outside the territory protected by the Khan, they were no longer safe. As they passed through what is now Turkey, the government took 4,000 gold coins from them.

Despite the loss of a large amount of their riches, the Polos kept enough of their goods to arrive home wealthy when they finally got back to Venice in 1295. Some historians believe that they sewed valuable gems into the inner linings of their coats so they would not be taken from them.

HOW DO WE KNOW ABOUT MARCO POLO?

Three years after Marco Polo came back, he was captured and thrown in prison for leading a Venetian ship into battle against the rival city of Genoa, Italy.

While he was in prison, he dictated all of his adventures to a man by the name of Rustichello, a fellow prisoner who was a writer of romance novels. By the time they were released from prison a year later, they had completed the book. It was called The Travels of Marco Polo.

The book made Marco a famous celebrity throughout Europe and his book was printed not only in Italian, but also in French and Latin.

Rustichello acted as a ghostwriter for Marco Polo and he was an amazing storyteller. The book included detailed descriptions of the royal palace at Xanadu and the city of Quinsai. These wonders of the Orient were so amazing that many readers didn't believe the stories were true. The citizens of Venice became convinced that the book was fiction and started to call it "Il Milione," which meant that they thought it contained a million lies.

Marco moved on with his life despite what others thought. He went back to his hometown of Venice and married. He and his wife had three daughters. For 25 years, he carried on the traditions of the family business.

Most modern historians believe the majority of the book is accurate, but a few believe that Marco Polo never set a foot into China. Marco Polo insisted that the book was true and said on his death bed on January 8, 1324, "I didn't tell even half of what I witnessed."

THE END OF KUBLAI KAHN'S REIGN

While Marco, his father, and his uncle were on their way back to Venice, the Great Khan died. The Mongol empire he had presided over went into quick decline.

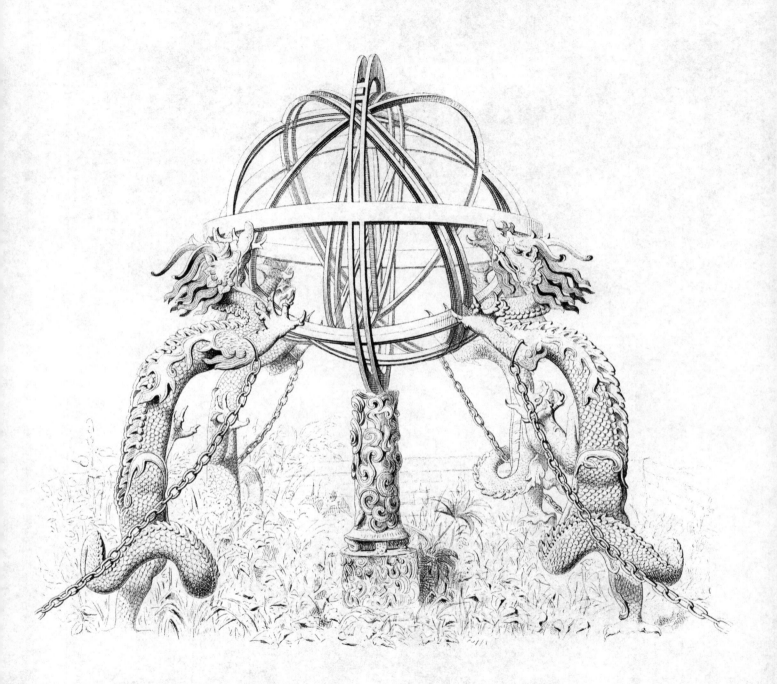

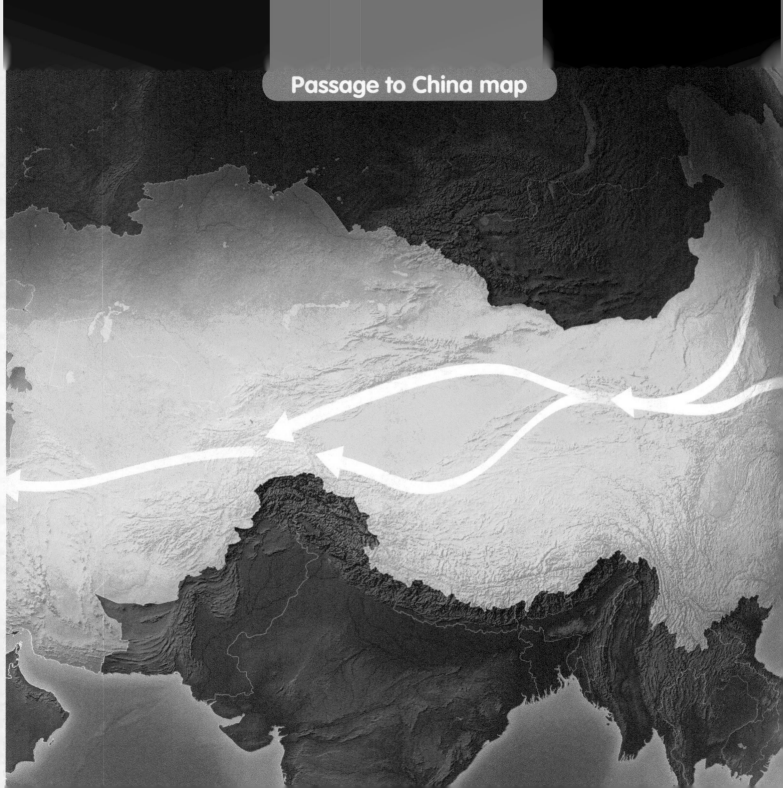

The Silk Road was no longer accessible as tribal groups reclaimed it and cut off this vital route that connected East to West. The passage to China was getting so dangerous that very few would dare the journey that Marco had made.

THE LEGACY OF MARCO POLO

In the many centuries that have passed since Marco Polo's death, he has received the praise he should have received during his lifetime. Researchers, explorers, and scholars have verified facts he recorded that no one else could have known at that time. It's possible that some of the stories included came through discussions Marco Polo had with other explorers.

In any event, his exciting adventures inspired many others to pursue the quest for new discoveries. When Christopher Columbus set out across the Atlantic Ocean, he had a copy of The Travels of Marco Polo with him.

Columbus never realized that the Khan's empire had already fallen by the time he set out on his travels. He had planned to follow Marco's same path. It was his intention to find a new path to the Orient and meet with the emperor who was now in Khan's position.

Awesome! Now you know more about the exciting life of Marco Polo. You can find more Historical Biography books from Baby Professor by searching the website of your favorite book retailer.

Visit

BABY PROFESSOR
EDUCATION KIDS

www.BabyProfessorBooks.com
to download Free Baby Professor eBooks
and view our catalog of new and exciting
Children's Books

CPSIA information can be obtained
at www.ICGtesting.com
Printed in the USA
BVHW091928020719
552533BV00009B/187/P